To:

Never Forget the Difference YOU'VE Made

♥

Live Your Best Life

Every. Single. Day.